Dream Life

daily journal

30 DAYS

to

JUMPSTART YOUR BEST LIFE

DENISE WALSH

Dream Life Daily Journal by Denise Walsh
1006 Cherry St SE
Grand Rapids, MI 49506
DeniseWalsh.com
hello@denisewalsh.com

Visit the author's website at DeniseWalsh.com and DreamLifeTool Kit.com.

International Standard Book Number: 978-1-71983-519-0

First edition

18 19 20 21 22 — 987654321
Printed in the United States of America

Introduction

> The secret of your success is determined by your daily agenda.
>
> John C. Maxwell

Your future is full of possibility. No matter how your life looks now—whether you are experiencing crazy levels of success, walking through your most challenging days, or are somewhere in between—you can improve your life and your way of living it simply by making adjustments to your daily routine. Beginning your morning with gratitude, prayer, meditation, reflection, and action is the best way to get centered so that you can decide how your day will go from a place of clarity.

The *Dream Life Daily Journal* contains a series of not-so-obvious exercises that will help you start your day right and bring you closer to creating the life that accomplishes all of your goals. Each day you'll learn how to create the space you need to first set your mind and heart and then make an action plan to ensure that each day is productive.

If you will spend twenty to thirty minutes on this each day, you'll learn how to:

- get aligned with the Holy Spirit and develop a positive state of mind through gratitude, prayer, meditation, and reflection;
- rewire your brain so you can see your Dream Life playing out in front of you now;
- create your daily action plan (a to-do list that is anything but mundane); and
- think creatively about health, relationships, and other areas of your life.

Over the course of this thirty-day journey, there will be lots of repetition. You will rewrite your goal daily. You will rewrite and repeat life-changing affirmations daily. You will make time each day imagining the life you have dreamed of. This is intentional. It takes twenty-one days to form a habit, and the goal here is to establish new habits and turn those practices into a lifestyle that will breed success. Resist the urge to skip these exercises because they are the same as what you did the day before. Trust me; the recitation of who and how you will be when you reach it, and the visualization of your Dream Life this month, will cement your dream and bring you closer to achieving it. The more solidly you can see yourself living your Dream Life, the more real it will become. You are creating new thought patterns and strengthening your identity, so consistency is key.

If, as you begin this journey, you discover that you need help connecting your big dreams with specific action items, or if you need to learn how to dream big and set actionable goals for the first time, I would encourage you to visit DreamLifeToolKit.com and download the *Dream Life Action Planner*. It works in tandem with the *Dream Life Daily Journal* to give you a step-by-step pathway toward your best life and lay a foundation for the pursuit of your passion. These materials are only two among many resources available at DreamLifeToolKit.com to help you in your journey.

My dream is for you to feel immense joy and live your Dream Life in every way, every day! That takes both a decision to begin this journey and your commitment to an ongoing growth process. Make this journal part of your morning routine, and it will serve as a daily action guide that will keep you on track, allow you to see real progress, help you reach that elusive next level, and break through whatever ceiling is holding you back.

It's time for you to enjoy the journey, my friends. Enjoy the day!

Day 1

Thoughts become words. Words become actions. Actions become habits. Habits become our destiny.

Morning Prayer

Thank You, God, for this amazing day. I love the life You've given me, and I know where I'm going because You are with me and give me strength. Thank You for the impact I am making in the world and people's lives today. Use me for Your purpose and Your glory, in Jesus' name. Amen.

Eyes Wide Open

Take a few moments to consider how God has made His presence known in your life lately. What prayers has He answered for you? How have you experienced Him in your life or surroundings?

_____

_____

_____

_____

_____

_____

Gratitude Game

Future Present

Imagine it is five years from now and you are writing yourself a letter.

Date the letter, and describe in it all the amazing adventures you have experienced in five years' time. Be as detailed and emotionally connected to your account as possible, and read your letter as often as you can. How do you feel when you read it back to yourself?

Prayer

This is a special place of hope, victory, and healing. It is your opportunity to ask the Holy Spirit to move in certain situations and relationships. Rather than filing your complaints, tell Him how you'd like these situations and relationships to look. Jot down four specific requests below, being careful to focus on asking Him for victory in these areas instead of simply listing grievances. Be sure to pay attention over time to how things change.

1
_____
_____
_____

2
_____
_____
_____

3
_____
_____
_____

4
_____
_____
_____

Meditation

You asked the Holy Spirit to move. Now listen for God's voice. You can add music or keep it silent. Make a goal to add more time to this section over the coming weeks.

Reflection

During your time of meditation, did you sense God speaking to you? What do you believe He is calling you to do? Do you feel excited? Conflicted? Peaceful? Was anyone brought to your mind? Did you get a new idea? Now is the time to write it all down!

My Current Dream Life Goal

Writing your goals down each day creates momentum over time. Use this space to write down the Dream Life Goal or other big goal you are working toward.

_____

_____

_____

_____

Affirmations

Daily affirmations are simple, positive statements declaring specific goals in their completed state. To get started, think about who you will be, how you will feel, and what your life will look like when your goal is complete. Then write several statements that agree with this outcome. A few examples are: I am a supportive and loving spouse and an engaged parent. I happily love myself exactly the way I am. I am earning $4,000 a month or more.

When you are done, read these affirmations out loud to yourself. You will do this every day until you truly believe it and then embody it.

I am _____

I am _____

I am _____

I am _____

Visualization

Cement your Dream Life Goal in your mind by picturing yourself achieving it. What will your life look like when your goal is completed? Notice any new details you can see today.

Dream Life Goal Action Items:

This to-do list is not about laundry, groceries, or baths for the kids. These are action-oriented steps for today that will move you toward your goals. Make sure they are all small enough to accomplish and check off your list today.

These action items should also be specific. For example, "work on project" is not specific enough, because your project might take weeks to complete. Break it down into pieces, such as "work on chapter 1," "call ten prospects," or "join a local meet-up group."

- ☐ _____
- ☐ _____
- ☐ _____

Dream Health Action Item:

List one health-conscious thing you plan to do today. Is it to improve your water intake? Make more time for exercise? Tweak your menu or your sleep time?

- ☐ _____

Dream Relationship Action Items:

What can you do today to be more intentional about important relationships? Text your spouse? Connect with a friend? Plan special times with each of your children?

- ☐ _____
- ☐ _____
- ☐ _____
- ☐ _____

Day 2

And now these three remain: faith, hope and love. But the greatest of these is love.

1 Corinthians 13:13

Morning Prayer

Thank You, God, for this amazing day. I love the life You've given me, and I know where I'm going because You are with me and give me strength. Thank You for the impact I am making in the world and people's lives today. Use me for Your purpose and Your glory, in Jesus' name. Amen.

Eyes Wide Open

Take a few moments to consider how God has made His presence known in your life lately. What prayers has He answered for you? How have you experienced Him in your life or surroundings?

_____

_____

_____

_____

_____

Gratitude Game
Appreciate All Things

Play what I like to call the "Aunt Francis and Uncle Frank Game." My aunt and uncle found something wonderfully joyful in everything they saw and experienced. You can do the same!

Here's how: Look around you. What can you appreciate in your immediate environment? If you're driving down the street, appreciate the trees, the squirrels, the weather, the traffic—anything and everything you get to experience. Appreciate all things. Start now by writing down all the little, yet amazing things that come to mind.

Prayer

This is a special place of hope, victory, and healing. It is your opportunity to ask the Holy Spirit to move in certain situations and relationships. Rather than filing your complaints, tell Him how you'd like these situations and relationships to look. Jot down four specific requests below, being careful to focus on asking Him for victory in these areas instead of simply listing grievances. Be sure to pay attention over time to how things change.

1

2

3

4

Meditation

You asked the Holy Spirit to move. Now listen for God's voice. You can add music or keep it silent. Make a goal to add more time to this section over the coming weeks.

Reflection

Did you sense God speaking to you? What do you believe He is calling you to do? Do you feel excited? Conflicted? Peaceful? Was anyone brought to your mind? Did you get a new idea? Now is the time to write it all down!

_____

_____

_____

_____

_____

_____

_____

_____

_____

_____

_____

_____

_____

_____

_____

_____

_____

Dream Life Goal

Writing your goals down each and every day creates momentum over time. Use this space to write down the Dream Life Goal or other big goal you are working toward.

_____

_____

_____

_____

_____

_____

Affirmations

Who will you be, how will you feel, and what will your life look like when your goal is complete? Write down the affirmations that correspond to the person you are becoming and the life you are creating. When you are done, read these affirmations out loud to yourself.

I am _____

I am _____

I am _____

I am _____

I am _____

Visualization

Cement your big goal in your mind by picturing yourself achieving it. What will your life look like when your goal is completed? Notice any new details you can see today.

Dream Life Goal Action Items:

Remember, this to-do list is not about laundry, groceries, or baths for the kids. These are action-oriented steps for today that will move you toward your goals. Make sure they are all small enough and specific enough to accomplish and check off your list today.

- [ ] _____
- [ ] _____
- [ ] _____
- [ ] _____
- [ ] _____

Dream Health Action Item:

List one health-conscious thing you plan to do today. Is it to improve your water intake? Make more time for exercise? Tweak your menu or your sleep time?

- [ ] _____

Dream Relationship Action Items:

What can you do today to be more intentional about important relationships? Text your spouse? Connect with a friend? Plan special times with each of your children?

- [ ] _____
- [ ] _____
- [ ] _____
- [ ] _____

Day 3

Gratitude is the healthiest of all human emotions. The more you express gratitude for what you have, the more likely you will have even more to express gratitude for.

Zig Ziglar

Morning Prayer

Thank You, God, for this amazing day. I love the life You've given me, and I know where I'm going because You are with me and give me strength. Thank You for the impact I am making in the world and people's lives today. Use me for Your purpose and Your glory, in Jesus' name. Amen.

Eyes Wide Open

Take a few moments to consider how God has made His presence known in your life lately. What prayers has He answered for you? How have you experienced Him in your life or surroundings?

_____

_____

_____

_____

_____

_____

_____

Gratitude Game

Appreciate All People

Make a conscious effort to really see and appreciate everyone you meet today.

Make eye contact. Say thank you. Ask them about their day and appreciate their role in helping your day go smoothly. Spend a minute writing about who you are grateful for and why. Try to focus on at least five people who help make your life better. How can you express what they mean to you?

1
_____

_____

_____

_____

2
_____

_____

_____

_____

3
_____

_____

_____

_____

4
_____

_____

_____

_____

5
_____

_____

_____

_____

Prayer

This is a special place of hope, victory, and healing. It is your opportunity to ask the Holy Spirit to move in certain situations and relationships. Rather than filing your complaints, tell Him how you'd like these situations and relationships to look. Jot down four specific requests below, being careful to focus on asking Him for victory in these areas instead of simply listing grievances. Be sure to pay attention over time to how things change.

1
\
\
\

2
\
\
\

3
\
\
\

4
\
\
\

Meditation

You asked the Holy Spirit to move. Now listen for God's voice. You can add music or keep it silent. Make a goal to add more time to this section over the coming weeks.

Reflection

Did you sense God speaking to you? What do you believe He is calling you to do? Do you feel excited? Conflicted? Peaceful? Was anyone brought to your mind? Did you get a new idea? Now is the time to write it all down!

Dream Life Goal

Writing your goals down each and every day creates momentum over time. Use this space to write down the Dream Life Goal or other big goal you are working toward.

_____

_____

_____

_____

_____

_____

Affirmations

Who will you be, how will you feel, and what will your life look like when your goal is complete? Write down the affirmations that correspond to the person you are becoming and the life you are creating. When you are done, read these affirmations out loud to yourself.

I am _____

I am _____

I am _____

I am _____

I am _____

Visualization

Cement your big goal in your mind by picturing yourself achieving it. What will your life look like when your goal is completed? Notice any new details you can see today.

Dream Life Goal Action Items:

Remember, this to-do list is not about laundry, groceries, or baths for the kids. These are action-oriented steps for today that will move you toward your goals. Make sure they are all small enough and specific enough to accomplish and check off your list today.

- ☐ _____
- ☐ _____
- ☐ _____
- ☐ _____
- ☐ _____

Dream Health Action Item:

List one health-conscious thing you plan to do today. Is it to improve your water intake? Make more time for exercise? Tweak your menu or your sleep time?

- ☐ _____

Dream Relationship Action Items:

What can you do today to be more intentional about important relationships? Text your spouse? Connect with a friend? Plan special times with each of your children?

- ☐ _____
- ☐ _____
- ☐ _____
- ☐ _____

Day 4

It's not that life has been easy, perfect, or exactly as expected. I just choose to be happy and grateful no matter how it all turns out.

Albert Einstein

Morning Prayer

Thank You, God, for this amazing day. I love the life You've given me, and I know where I'm going because You are with me and give me strength. Thank You for the impact I am making in the world and people's lives today. Use me for Your purpose and Your glory, in Jesus' name. Amen.

Eyes Wide Open

Take a few moments to consider how God has made His presence known in your life lately. What prayers has He answered for you? How have you experienced Him in your life or surroundings?

_____

_____

_____

_____

_____

_____

_____

Gratitude Game

Let's Get Away

Pretend you're on vacation.

Whatever you do this day, do it because you want to, because you choose to, and you're having fun doing it. Use this space to write about what this vacation day would look and feel like, and imagine yourself being over-the-top grateful for the experience.

Prayer

This is a special place of hope, victory, and healing. It is your opportunity to ask the Holy Spirit to move in certain situations and relationships. Rather than filing your complaints, tell Him how you'd like these situations and relationships to look. Jot down four specific requests below, being careful to focus on asking Him for victory in these areas instead of simply listing grievances. Be sure to pay attention over time to how things change.

1
_____

_____

_____

2
_____

_____

_____

3
_____

_____

_____

4
_____

_____

_____

Meditation

You asked the Holy Spirit to move. Now listen for God's voice. You can add music or keep it silent. Make a goal to add more time to this section over the coming weeks.

Reflection

Did you sense God speaking to you? What do you believe He is calling you to do? Do you feel excited? Conflicted? Peaceful? Was anyone brought to your mind? Did you get a new idea? Now is the time to write it all down!

_____

_____

_____

_____

_____

_____

_____

_____

_____

_____

_____

_____

_____

_____

_____

_____

_____

Dream Life Goal

Writing your goals down each and every day creates momentum over time. Use this space to write down the Dream Life Goal or other big goal you are working toward.

_____

_____

_____

_____

_____

_____

Affirmations

Who will you be, how will you feel, and what will your life look like when your goal is complete? Write down the affirmations that correspond to the person you are becoming and the life you are creating. When you are done, read these affirmations out loud to yourself.

I am _____

I am _____

I am _____

I am _____

I am _____

Visualization

Cement your big goal in your mind by picturing yourself achieving it. What will your life look like when your goal is completed? Notice any new details you can see today.

Dream Life Goal Action Items:

Remember, this to-do list is not about laundry, groceries, or baths for the kids. These are action-oriented steps for today that will move you toward your goals. Make sure they are all small enough and specific enough to accomplish and check off your list today.

- ☐ _____
- ☐ _____
- ☐ _____
- ☐ _____
- ☐ _____

Dream Health Action Item:

List one health-conscious thing you plan to do today. Is it to improve your water intake? Make more time for exercise? Tweak your menu or your sleep time?

- ☐ _____

Dream Relationship Action Items:

What can you do today to be more intentional about important relationships? Text your spouse? Connect with a friend? Plan special times with each of your children?

- ☐ _____
- ☐ _____
- ☐ _____
- ☐ _____

Day 5

I am the LORD, the God of all mankind. Is anything too hard for me?

Jeremiah 32:27

Morning Prayer

Thank You, God, for this amazing day. I love the life You've given me, and I know where I'm going because You are with me and give me strength. Thank You for the impact I am making in the world and people's lives today. Use me for Your purpose and Your glory, in Jesus' name. Amen.

Eyes Wide Open

Take a few moments to consider how God has made His presence known in your life lately. What prayers has He answered for you? How have you experienced Him in your life or surroundings?

_____

_____

_____

_____

Gratitude Game

Promises Kept

Think back over the last five to ten years of your life, or beyond. How has God been faithful to you in that time? Were there any challenging situations in which He seemed absent, but later you realized He was clearly working things together for your ultimate benefit?

Now, think back to how you felt in the midst of that situation, before you saw and felt God move on your behalf. Right a letter of encouragement to yourself in that season. Include what you needed to hear at the time to persevere and the perspective you have now that you are on the other side. When you encounter another season in which God seems silent, reread this letter as a reminder of God's faithfulness.

Prayer

This is a special place of hope, victory, and healing. It is your opportunity to ask the Holy Spirit to move in certain situations and relationships. Rather than filing your complaints, tell Him how you'd like these situations and relationships to look. Jot down four specific requests below, being careful to focus on asking Him for victory in these areas instead of simply listing grievances. Be sure to pay attention over time to how things change.

1

2

3

4

Meditation

You asked the Holy Spirit to move. Now listen for God's voice. You can add music or keep it silent. Make a goal to add more time to this section over the coming weeks.

Reflection

Did you sense God speaking to you? What do you believe He is calling you to do? Do you feel excited? Conflicted? Peaceful? Was anyone brought to your mind? Did you get a new idea? Now is the time to write it all down!

_____

_____

_____

_____

_____

_____

_____

_____

_____

_____

_____

_____

_____

_____

_____

_____

_____

Dream Life Goal

Writing your goals down each and every day creates momentum over time. Use this space to write down the Dream Life Goal or other big goal you are working toward.

_____

_____

_____

_____

_____

_____

Affirmations

Who will you be, how will you feel, and what will your life look like when your goal is complete? Write down the affirmations that correspond to the person you are becoming and the life you are creating. When you are done, read these affirmations out loud to yourself.

I am _____

I am _____

I am _____

I am _____

I am _____

Visualization

Cement your big goal in your mind by picturing yourself achieving it. What will your life look like when your goal is completed? Notice any new details you can see today.

Dream Life Goal Action Items:

Remember, this to-do list is not about laundry, groceries, or baths for the kids. These are action-oriented steps for today that will move you toward your goals. Make sure they are all small enough and specific enough to accomplish and check off your list today.

- ☐ _____
- ☐ _____
- ☐ _____
- ☐ _____
- ☐ _____

Dream Health Action Item:

List one health-conscious thing you plan to do today. Is it to improve your water intake? Make more time for exercise? Tweak your menu or your sleep time?

- ☐ _____

Dream Relationship Action Items:

What can you do today to be more intentional about important relationships? Text your spouse? Connect with a friend? Plan special times with each of your children?

- ☐ _____
- ☐ _____
- ☐ _____
- ☐ _____

Day 6

Unbelief starves the soul; faith finds food in famine.

Richard Cecil

Morning Prayer

Thank You, God, for this amazing day. I love the life You've given me, and I know where I'm going because You are with me and give me strength. Thank You for the impact I am making in the world and people's lives today. Use me for Your purpose and Your glory, in Jesus' name. Amen.

Eyes Wide Open

Take a few moments to consider how God has made His presence known in your life lately. What prayers has He answered for you? How have you experienced Him in your life or surroundings?

_____

_____

_____

_____

_____

_____

Gratitude Game

Everything Is Awesome!

Whatever happens today, call it awesome—and mean it!

Spend a minute describing what today will look like for you when everything is going right.

Prayer

This is a special place of hope, victory, and healing. It is your opportunity to ask the Holy Spirit to move in certain situations and relationships. Rather than filing your complaints, tell Him how you'd like these situations and relationships to look. Jot down four specific requests below, being careful to focus on asking Him for victory in these areas instead of simply listing grievances. Be sure to pay attention over time to how things change.

1

2

3

4

Meditation

You asked the Holy Spirit to move. Now listen for God's voice. You can add music or keep it silent. Make a goal to add more time to this section over the coming weeks.

Reflection

Did you sense God speaking to you? What do you believe He is calling you to do? Do you feel excited? Conflicted? Peaceful? Was anyone brought to your mind? Did you get a new idea? Now is the time to write it all down!

Dream Life Goal

Writing your goals down each and every day creates momentum over time. Use this space to write down the Dream Life Goal or other big goal you are working toward.

_____

_____

_____

_____

_____

_____

Affirmations

Who will you be, how will you feel, and what will your life look like when your goal is complete? Write down the affirmations that correspond to the person you are becoming and the life you are creating. When you are done, read these affirmations out loud to yourself.

I am _____

I am _____

I am _____

I am _____

I am _____

Visualization

Cement your big goal in your mind by picturing yourself achieving it. What will your life look like when your goal is completed? Notice any new details you can see today.

Dream Life Goal Action Items:

Remember, this to-do list is not about laundry, groceries, or baths for the kids. These are action-oriented steps for today that will move you toward your goals. Make sure they are all small enough and specific enough to accomplish and check off your list today.

- [ ] _____
- [ ] _____
- [ ] _____
- [ ] _____
- [ ] _____

Dream Health Action Item:

List one health-conscious thing you plan to do today. Is it to improve your water intake? Make more time for exercise? Tweak your menu or your sleep time?

- [ ] _____

Dream Relationship Action Items:

What can you do today to be more intentional about important relationships? Text your spouse? Connect with a friend? Plan special times with each of your children?

- [ ] _____
- [ ] _____
- [ ] _____
- [ ] _____

Day 7

Everything is possible for one who believes.

Mark 9:23

Morning Prayer

Thank You, God, for this amazing day. I love the life You've given me, and I know where I'm going because You are with me and give me strength. Thank You for the impact I am making in the world and people's lives today. Use me for Your purpose and Your glory, in Jesus' name. Amen.

Eyes Wide Open

Take a few moments to consider how God has made His presence known in your life lately. What prayers has He answered for you? How have you experienced Him in your life or surroundings?

_____

_____

_____

_____

_____

_____

Gratitude Game

Be a Broken Record

Plan to say thank you to everyone you encounter today. Do it with over-the-top smiles and in-your-face, gushy, all-in thankfulness, over and over again.

Before you continue on with your day, take a few moments to consider who in your life adds value and write down how you will make it a point to thank them.

Prayer

This is a special place of hope, victory, and healing. It is your opportunity to ask the Holy Spirit to move in certain situations and relationships. Rather than filing your complaints, tell Him how you'd like these situations and relationships to look. Jot down four specific requests below, being careful to focus on asking Him for victory in these areas instead of simply listing grievances. Be sure to pay attention over time to how things change.

1

2

3

4

Meditation

You asked the Holy Spirit to move. Now listen for God's voice. You can add music or keep it silent. Make a goal to add more time to this section over the coming weeks.

Reflection

Did you sense God speaking to you? What do you believe He is calling you to do? Do you feel excited? Conflicted? Peaceful? Was anyone brought to your mind? Did you get a new idea? Now is the time to write it all down!

Dream Life Goal

Writing your goals down each and every day creates momentum over time. Use this space to write down the Dream Life Goal or other big goal you are working toward.

_____

_____

_____

_____

_____

_____

Affirmations

Who will you be, how will you feel, and what will your life look like when your goal is complete? Write down the affirmations that correspond to the person you are becoming and the life you are creating. When you are done, read these affirmations out loud to yourself.

I am _____

I am _____

I am _____

I am _____

I am _____

Visualization

Cement your big goal in your mind by picturing yourself achieving it. What will your life look like when your goal is completed? Notice any new details you can see today.

Dream Life Goal Action Items:

Remember, this to-do list is not about laundry, groceries, or baths for the kids. These are action-oriented steps for today that will move you toward your goals. Make sure they are all small enough and specific enough to accomplish and check off your list today.

- [ ] _____
- [ ] _____
- [ ] _____
- [ ] _____
- [ ] _____

Dream Health Action Item:

List one health-conscious thing you plan to do today. Is it to improve your water intake? Make more time for exercise? Tweak your menu or your sleep time?

- [ ] _____

Dream Relationship Action Items:

What can you do today to be more intentional about important relationships? Text your spouse? Connect with a friend? Plan special times with each of your children?

- [ ] _____
- [ ] _____
- [ ] _____
- [ ] _____

Day 8

Quiet your mind, and your soul
will speak.

Morning Prayer

Thank You, God, for this amazing day. I love the life You've given me, and I know where I'm going because You are with me and give me strength. Thank You for the impact I am making in the world and people's lives today. Use me for Your purpose and Your glory, in Jesus' name. Amen.

Eyes Wide Open

Take a few moments to consider how God has made His presence known in your life lately. What prayers has He answered for you? How have you experienced Him in your life or surroundings?

_____

_____

_____

_____

_____

_____

Gratitude Game

Create Your Story

Harness the power of a decision.

Whatever is happening in your life right now, write down the rest of the story as you desire it to be. Decide that your story is easy, fun, and that in the end everything will go your way.

Prayer

This is a special place of hope, victory, and healing. It is your opportunity to ask the Holy Spirit to move in certain situations and relationships. Rather than filing your complaints, tell Him how you'd like these situations and relationships to look. Jot down four specific requests below, being careful to focus on asking Him for victory in these areas instead of simply listing grievances. Be sure to pay attention over time to how things change.

1
_____
_____
_____

2
_____
_____
_____

3
_____
_____
_____

4
_____
_____
_____

Meditation

You asked the Holy Spirit to move. Now listen for God's voice. You can add music or keep it silent. Make a goal to add more time to this section over the coming weeks.

Reflection

Did you sense God speaking to you? What do you believe He is calling you to do? Do you feel excited? Conflicted? Peaceful? Was anyone brought to your mind? Did you get a new idea? Now is the time to write it all down!

_____

_____

_____

_____

_____

_____

_____

_____

_____

_____

_____

_____

_____

_____

_____

_____

_____

Dream Life Goal

Writing your goals down each and every day creates momentum over time. Use this space to write down the Dream Life Goal or other big goal you are working toward.

_____

_____

_____

_____

_____

Affirmations

Who will you be, how will you feel, and what will your life look like when your goal is complete? Write down the affirmations that correspond to the person you are becoming and the life you are creating. When you are done, read these affirmations out loud to yourself.

I am _____

I am _____

I am _____

I am _____

I am _____

Visualization

Cement your big goal in your mind by picturing yourself achieving it. What will your life look like when your goal is completed? Notice any new details you can see today.

Dream Life Goal Action Items:

Remember, this to-do list is not about laundry, groceries, or baths for the kids. These are action-oriented steps for today that will move you toward your goals. Make sure they are all small enough and specific enough to accomplish and check off your list today.

- [ ] _____
- [ ] _____
- [ ] _____
- [ ] _____
- [ ] _____

Dream Health Action Item:

List one health-conscious thing you plan to do today. Is it to improve your water intake? Make more time for exercise? Tweak your menu or your sleep time?

- [ ] _____

Dream Relationship Action Items:

What can you do today to be more intentional about important relationships? Text your spouse? Connect with a friend? Plan special times with each of your children?

- [ ] _____
- [ ] _____
- [ ] _____
- [ ] _____

Day 9

Prayer is when you talk to God. Meditation is when God talks to you.

Morning Prayer

Thank You, God, for this amazing day. I love the life You've given me, and I know where I'm going because You are with me and give me strength. Thank You for the impact I am making in the world and people's lives today. Use me for Your purpose and Your glory, in Jesus' name. Amen.

Eyes Wide Open

Take a few moments to consider how God has made His presence known in your life lately. What prayers has He answered for you? How have you experienced Him in your life or surroundings?

_____

_____

_____

_____

_____

_____

_____

Gratitude Game

X-ray Vision

Today, choose to see people the way God does—for their potential and purpose. Picture them three steps ahead of where they see themselves and treat them like they're already there.

In the journaling space on the next page, consider who you can speak belief into today, and how you will show them this love.

Prayer

This is a special place of hope, victory, and healing. It is your opportunity to ask the Holy Spirit to move in certain situations and relationships. Rather than filing your complaints, tell Him how you'd like these situations and relationships to look. Jot down four specific requests below, being careful to focus on asking Him for victory in these areas instead of simply listing grievances. Be sure to pay attention over time to how things change.

1
_____

_____

_____

2
_____

_____

_____

3
_____

_____

_____

4
_____

_____

_____

Meditation

You asked the Holy Spirit to move. Now listen for God's voice. You can add music or keep it silent. Make a goal to add more time to this section over the coming weeks.

Reflection

Did you sense God speaking to you? What do you believe He is calling you to do? Do you feel excited? Conflicted? Peaceful? Was anyone brought to your mind? Did you get a new idea? Now is the time to write it all down!

_____

_____

_____

_____

_____

_____

_____

_____

_____

_____

_____

_____

_____

_____

_____

_____

Dream Life Goal

Writing your goals down each and every day creates momentum over time. Use this space to write down the Dream Life Goal or other big goal you are working toward.

_____

_____

_____

_____

_____

_____

Affirmations

Who will you be, how will you feel, and what will your life look like when your goal is complete? Write down the affirmations that correspond to the person you are becoming and the life you are creating. When you are done, read these affirmations out loud to yourself.

I am _____

I am _____

I am _____

I am _____

I am _____

Visualization

Cement your big goal in your mind by picturing yourself achieving it. What will your life look like when your goal is completed? Notice any new details you can see today.

Dream Life Goal Action Items:

Remember, this to-do list is not about laundry, groceries, or baths for the kids. These are action-oriented steps for today that will move you toward your goals. Make sure they are all small enough and specific enough to accomplish and check off your list today.

- ☐ _____
- ☐ _____
- ☐ _____
- ☐ _____
- ☐ _____

Dream Health Action Item:

List one health-conscious thing you plan to do today. Is it to improve your water intake? Make more time for exercise? Tweak your menu or your sleep time?

- ☐ _____

Dream Relationship Action Items:

What can you do today to be more intentional about important relationships? Text your spouse? Connect with a friend? Plan special times with each of your children?

- ☐ _____
- ☐ _____
- ☐ _____
- ☐ _____

Day 10

Now to him who is able to do immeasurably more than all we ask or imagine, according to his power that is at work within us.

Ephesians 3:20

Morning Prayer

Thank You, God, for this amazing day. I love the life You've given me, and I know where I'm going because You are with me and give me strength. Thank You for the impact I am making in the world and people's lives today. Use me for Your purpose and Your glory, in Jesus' name. Amen.

Eyes Wide Open

Take a few moments to consider how God has made His presence known in your life lately. What prayers has He answered for you? How have you experienced Him in your life or surroundings?

_____

_____

_____

_____

_____

_____

Gratitude Game

Ask Big

Be grateful today for the exciting, special, and purposeful plans God has for your life. He has given you immeasurably more than you could dream of asking for. Thank Him for it!

Spend a moment writing a thank-you note to God for life, love, and the adventure that surrounds you.

Prayer

This is a special place of hope, victory, and healing. It is your opportunity to ask the Holy Spirit to move in certain situations and relationships. Rather than filing your complaints, tell Him how you'd like these situations and relationships to look. Jot down four specific requests below, being careful to focus on asking Him for victory in these areas instead of simply listing grievances. Be sure to pay attention over time to how things change.

1
_____
_____
_____

2
_____
_____
_____

3
_____
_____
_____

4
_____
_____
_____

Meditation

You asked the Holy Spirit to move. Now listen for God's voice. You can add music or keep it silent. Make a goal to add more time to this section over the coming weeks.

Reflection

Did you sense God speaking to you? What do you believe He is calling you to do? Do you feel excited? Conflicted? Peaceful? Was anyone brought to your mind? Did you get a new idea? Now is the time to write it all down!

_____

_____

_____

_____

_____

_____

_____

_____

_____

_____

_____

_____

_____

_____

_____

_____

_____

Dream Life Goal

Writing your goals down each and every day creates momentum over time. Use this space to write down the Dream Life Goal or other big goal you are working toward.

_____

_____

_____

_____

_____

_____

Affirmations

Who will you be, how will you feel, and what will your life look like when your goal is complete? Write down the affirmations that correspond to the person you are becoming and the life you are creating. When you are done, read these affirmations out loud to yourself.

I am _____

I am _____

I am _____

I am _____

I am _____

Visualization

Cement your big goal in your mind by picturing yourself achieving it. What will your life look like when your goal is completed? Notice any new details you can see today.

Dream Life Goal Action Items:

Remember, this to-do list is not about laundry, groceries, or baths for the kids. These are action-oriented steps for today that will move you toward your goals. Make sure they are all small enough and specific enough to accomplish and check off your list today.

- [ ] _____
- [ ] _____
- [ ] _____
- [ ] _____
- [ ] _____

Dream Health Action Item:

List one health-conscious thing you plan to do today. Is it to improve your water intake? Make more time for exercise? Tweak your menu or your sleep time?

- [ ] _____

Dream Relationship Action Items:

What can you do today to be more intentional about important relationships? Text your spouse? Connect with a friend? Plan special times with each of your children?

- [ ] _____
- [ ] _____
- [ ] _____
- [ ] _____

Day 11

Call on me and come and pray to me, and I will listen to you.

Jeremiah 29:12

Morning Prayer

Thank You, God, for this amazing day. I love the life You've given me, and I know where I'm going because You are with me and give me strength. Thank You for the impact I am making in the world and people's lives today. Use me for Your purpose and Your glory, in Jesus' name. Amen.

Eyes Wide Open

Take a few moments to consider how God has made His presence known in your life lately. What prayers has He answered for you? How have you experienced Him in your life or surroundings?

_____

_____

_____

_____

_____

_____

Gratitude Game

It's My Lucky Day!

Decide that 1) today will be an awesome day, 2) you are a "luck magnet," and 3) more than you ever thought possible, good things are happening in your life.

Write down what today will look like when everything goes right.

Prayer

This is a special place of hope, victory, and healing. It is your opportunity to ask the Holy Spirit to move in certain situations and relationships. Rather than filing your complaints, tell Him how you'd like these situations and relationships to look. Jot down four specific requests below, being careful to focus on asking Him for victory in these areas instead of simply listing grievances. Be sure to pay attention over time to how things change.

1
_____

_____

_____

2
_____

_____

_____

3
_____

_____

_____

4
_____

_____

_____

Meditation

You asked the Holy Spirit to move. Now listen for God's voice. You can add music or keep it silent. Make a goal to add more time to this section over the coming weeks.

Reflection

Did you sense God speaking to you? What do you believe He is calling you to do? Do you feel excited? Conflicted? Peaceful? Was anyone brought to your mind? Did you get a new idea? Now is the time to write it all down!

Dream Life Goal

Writing your goals down each and every day creates momentum over time. Use this space to write down the Dream Life Goal or other big goal you are working toward.

_____

_____

_____

_____

_____

Affirmations

Who will you be, how will you feel, and what will your life look like when your goal is complete? Write down the affirmations that correspond to the person you are becoming and the life you are creating. When you are done, read these affirmations out loud to yourself.

I am _____

I am _____

I am _____

I am _____

I am _____

Visualization

Cement your big goal in your mind by picturing yourself achieving it. What will your life look like when your goal is completed? Notice any new details you can see today.

Dream Life Goal Action Items:

Remember, this to-do list is not about laundry, groceries, or baths for the kids. These are action-oriented steps for today that will move you toward your goals. Make sure they are all small enough and specific enough to accomplish and check off your list today.

- ☐ _____
- ☐ _____
- ☐ _____
- ☐ _____
- ☐ _____

Dream Health Action Item:

List one health-conscious thing you plan to do today. Is it to improve your water intake? Make more time for exercise? Tweak your menu or your sleep time?

- ☐ _____

Dream Relationship Action Items:

What can you do today to be more intentional about important relationships? Text your spouse? Connect with a friend? Plan special times with each of your children?

- ☐ _____
- ☐ _____
- ☐ _____
- ☐ _____

Day 12

Some wake up to an alarm. Others wake up to a calling.

Morning Prayer

Thank You, God, for this amazing day. I love the life You've given me, and I know where I'm going because You are with me and give me strength. Thank You for the impact I am making in the world and people's lives today. Use me for Your purpose and Your glory, in Jesus' name. Amen.

Eyes Wide Open

Take a few moments to consider how God has made His presence known in your life lately. What prayers has He answered for you? How have you experienced Him in your life or surroundings?

_____

_____

_____

_____

_____

_____

Gratitude Game

Sore Cheeks

Write down your daily agenda, and imagine yourself smiling throughout every task. Smile so often today that your cheeks are sore by dinner time!

Prayer

This is a special place of hope, victory, and healing. It is your opportunity to ask the Holy Spirit to move in certain situations and relationships. Rather than filing your complaints, tell Him how you'd like these situations and relationships to look. Jot down four specific requests below, being careful to focus on asking Him for victory in these areas instead of simply listing grievances. Be sure to pay attention over time to how things change.

1 _____

_____

_____

2 _____

_____

_____

3 _____

_____

_____

4 _____

_____

_____

Meditation

You asked the Holy Spirit to move. Now listen for God's voice. You can add music or keep it silent. Make a goal to add more time to this section over the coming weeks.

Reflection

Did you sense God speaking to you? What do you believe He is calling you to do? Do you feel excited? Conflicted? Peaceful? Was anyone brought to your mind? Did you get a new idea? Now is the time to write it all down!

Dream Life Goal

Writing your goals down each and every day creates momentum over time. Use this space to write down the Dream Life Goal or other big goal you are working toward.

_____

_____

_____

_____

_____

_____

Affirmations

Who will you be, how will you feel, and what will your life look like when your goal is complete? Write down the affirmations that correspond to the person you are becoming and the life you are creating. When you are done, read these affirmations out loud to yourself.

I am _____

I am _____

I am _____

I am _____

I am _____

Visualization

Cement your big goal in your mind by picturing yourself achieving it. What will your life look like when your goal is completed? Notice any new details you can see today.

Dream Life Goal Action Items:

Remember, this to-do list is not about laundry, groceries, or baths for the kids. These are action-oriented steps for today that will move you toward your goals. Make sure they are all small enough and specific enough to accomplish and check off your list today.

- [ ] _____
- [ ] _____
- [ ] _____
- [ ] _____
- [ ] _____

Dream Health Action Item:

List one health-conscious thing you plan to do today. Is it to improve your water intake? Make more time for exercise? Tweak your menu or your sleep time?

- [ ] _____

Dream Relationship Action Items:

What can you do today to be more intentional about important relationships? Text your spouse? Connect with a friend? Plan special times with each of your children?

- [ ] _____
- [ ] _____
- [ ] _____
- [ ] _____

Day 13

"For I know the plans I have for you," declares the LORD, "plans to prosper you and not to harm you, plans to give you hope and a future."

Jeremiah 29:11

Morning Prayer

Thank You, God, for this amazing day. I love the life You've given me, and I know where I'm going because You are with me and give me strength. Thank You for the impact I am making in the world and people's lives today. Use me for Your purpose and Your glory, in Jesus' name. Amen.

Eyes Wide Open

Take a few moments to consider how God has made His presence known in your life lately. What prayers has He answered for you? How have you experienced Him in your life or surroundings?

_____

_____

_____

_____

_____

_____

_____

Gratitude Game

It Was a Success!

Think of something you finished that made you proud. Describe your accomplishment and how you felt after achieving it.

Prayer

This is a special place of hope, victory, and healing. It is your opportunity to ask the Holy Spirit to move in certain situations and relationships. Rather than filing your complaints, tell Him how you'd like these situations and relationships to look. Jot down four specific requests below, being careful to focus on asking Him for victory in these areas instead of simply listing grievances. Be sure to pay attention over time to how things change.

1

_____

_____

_____

2

_____

_____

_____

3

_____

_____

_____

4

_____

_____

_____

Meditation

You asked the Holy Spirit to move. Now listen for God's voice. You can add music or keep it silent. Make a goal to add more time to this section over the coming weeks.

Reflection

Did you sense God speaking to you? What do you believe He is calling you to do? Do you feel excited? Conflicted? Peaceful? Was anyone brought to your mind? Did you get a new idea? Now is the time to write it all down!

Dream Life Goal

Writing your goals down each and every day creates momentum over time. Use this space to write down the Dream Life Goal or other big goal you are working toward.

_____

_____

_____

_____

_____

_____

Affirmations

Who will you be, how will you feel, and what will your life look like when your goal is complete? Write down the affirmations that correspond to the person you are becoming and the life you are creating. When you are done, read these affirmations out loud to yourself.

I am _____

I am _____

I am _____

I am _____

I am _____

Visualization

Cement your big goal in your mind by picturing yourself achieving it. What will your life look like when your goal is completed? Notice any new details you can see today.

Dream Life Goal Action Items:

Remember, this to-do list is not about laundry, groceries, or baths for the kids. These are action-oriented steps for today that will move you toward your goals. Make sure they are all small enough and specific enough to accomplish and check off your list today.

- ☐ _____
- ☐ _____
- ☐ _____
- ☐ _____
- ☐ _____

Dream Health Action Item:

List one health-conscious thing you plan to do today. Is it to improve your water intake? Make more time for exercise? Tweak your menu or your sleep time?

- ☐ _____

Dream Relationship Action Items:

What can you do today to be more intentional about important relationships? Text your spouse? Connect with a friend? Plan special times with each of your children?

- ☐ _____
- ☐ _____
- ☐ _____
- ☐ _____

Day 14

Be fearless in the pursuit of what sets your soul on fire.

Jennifer Lee

Morning Prayer

Thank You, God, for this amazing day. I love the life You've given me, and I know where I'm going because You are with me and give me strength. Thank You for the impact I am making in the world and people's lives today. Use me for Your purpose and Your glory, in Jesus' name. Amen.

Eyes Wide Open

Take a few moments to consider how God has made His presence known in your life lately. What prayers has He answered for you? How have you experienced Him in your life or surroundings?

_____

_____

_____

_____

_____

_____

Gratitude Game
Thank You!

Think of at least three people who regularly enrich your life. How do they make your life better? How have they made you better?

After writing out your thoughts, text, call, or message these people to let them know how grateful you are for their love and support.

Prayer

This is a special place of hope, victory, and healing. It is your opportunity to ask the Holy Spirit to move in certain situations and relationships. Rather than filing your complaints, tell Him how you'd like these situations and relationships to look. Jot down four specific requests below, being careful to focus on asking Him for victory in these areas instead of simply listing grievances. Be sure to pay attention over time to how things change.

1
_____

_____

_____

2
_____

_____

_____

3
_____

_____

_____

4
_____

_____

_____

Meditation

You asked the Holy Spirit to move. Now listen for God's voice. You can add music or keep it silent. Make a goal to add more time to this section over the coming weeks.

Reflection

Did you sense God speaking to you? What do you believe He is calling you to do? Do you feel excited? Conflicted? Peaceful? Was anyone brought to your mind? Did you get a new idea? Now is the time to write it all down!

Dream Life Goal

Writing your goals down each and every day creates momentum over time. Use this space to write down the Dream Life Goal or other big goal you are working toward.

_____

_____

_____

_____

_____

Affirmations

Who will you be, how will you feel, and what will your life look like when your goal is complete? Write down the affirmations that correspond to the person you are becoming and the life you are creating. When you are done, read these affirmations out loud to yourself.

I am _____

I am _____

I am _____

I am _____

I am _____

Visualization

Cement your big goal in your mind by picturing yourself achieving it. What will your life look like when your goal is completed? Notice any new details you can see today.

Dream Life Goal Action Items:

Remember, this to-do list is not about laundry, groceries, or baths for the kids. These are action-oriented steps for today that will move you toward your goals. Make sure they are all small enough and specific enough to accomplish and check off your list today.

- ☐ _____
- ☐ _____
- ☐ _____
- ☐ _____
- ☐ _____

Dream Health Action Item:

List one health-conscious thing you plan to do today. Is it to improve your water intake? Make more time for exercise? Tweak your menu or your sleep time?

- ☐ _____

Dream Relationship Action Items:

What can you do today to be more intentional about important relationships? Text your spouse? Connect with a friend? Plan special times with each of your children?

- ☐ _____
- ☐ _____
- ☐ _____
- ☐ _____

Day 15

Repeat after me: "Everything is working out for my highest benefit."

Morning Prayer

Thank You, God, for this amazing day. I love the life You've given me, and I know where I'm going because You are with me and give me strength. Thank You for the impact I am making in the world and people's lives today. Use me for Your purpose and Your glory, in Jesus' name. Amen.

Eyes Wide Open

Take a few moments to consider how God has made His presence known in your life lately. What prayers has He answered for you? How have you experienced Him in your life or surroundings?

_____

_____

_____

_____

_____

_____

Gratitude Game

Hugs!

All of us need hugs every single day. Make it a goal to share at least five hugs with family and friends today.

Is it easy or hard for you to give and receive hugs? If it is easy for you, use this space to journal about how being close to friends and family makes you feel and what it represents for you. If the thought of hugging others is challenging for you, make a plan for reaching out to others with different types of platonic touch.

Prayer

This is a special place of hope, victory, and healing. It is your opportunity to ask the Holy Spirit to move in certain situations and relationships. Rather than filing your complaints, tell Him how you'd like these situations and relationships to look. Jot down four specific requests below, being careful to focus on asking Him for victory in these areas instead of simply listing grievances. Be sure to pay attention over time to how things change.

1
_____

_____

_____

2
_____

_____

_____

3
_____

_____

_____

4
_____

_____

_____

Meditation

You asked the Holy Spirit to move. Now listen for God's voice. You can add music or keep it silent. Make a goal to add more time to this section over the coming weeks.

Reflection

Did you sense God speaking to you? What do you believe He is calling you to do? Do you feel excited? Conflicted? Peaceful? Was anyone brought to your mind? Did you get a new idea? Now is the time to write it all down!

_____

_____

_____

_____

_____

_____

_____

_____

_____

_____

_____

_____

_____

_____

_____

_____

_____

Dream Life Goal

Writing your goals down each and every day creates momentum over time. Use this space to write down the Dream Life Goal or other big goal you are working toward.

_____

_____

_____

_____

_____

_____

Affirmations

Who will you be, how will you feel, and what will your life look like when your goal is complete? Write down the affirmations that correspond to the person you are becoming and the life you are creating. When you are done, read these affirmations out loud to yourself.

I am _____

I am _____

I am _____

I am _____

I am _____

Visualization

Cement your big goal in your mind by picturing yourself achieving it. What will your life look like when your goal is completed? Notice any new details you can see today.

Dream Life Goal Action Items:

Remember, this to-do list is not about laundry, groceries, or baths for the kids. These are action-oriented steps for today that will move you toward your goals. Make sure they are all small enough and specific enough to accomplish and check off your list today.

- ☐ _____
- ☐ _____
- ☐ _____
- ☐ _____
- ☐ _____

Dream Health Action Item:

List one health-conscious thing you plan to do today. Is it to improve your water intake? Make more time for exercise? Tweak your menu or your sleep time?

- ☐ _____

Dream Relationship Action Items:

What can you do today to be more intentional about important relationships? Text your spouse? Connect with a friend? Plan special times with each of your children?

- ☐ _____
- ☐ _____
- ☐ _____
- ☐ _____

Day 16

Happiness is an inside job.

Morning Prayer

Thank You, God, for this amazing day. I love the life You've given me, and I know where I'm going because You are with me and give me strength. Thank You for the impact I am making in the world and people's lives today. Use me for Your purpose and Your glory, in Jesus' name. Amen.

Eyes Wide Open

Take a few moments to consider how God has made His presence known in your life lately. What prayers has He answered for you? How have you experienced Him in your life or surroundings?

_____

_____

_____

_____

_____

_____

Gratitude Game
Gratitude Walk

Walk around your house, inside and out, and observe what you love and possibly take for granted about it.

Observe thoughtfully, taking it all in—family photos, household gadgets, bedrooms, birds, trees, neighbors, everything! With intentionality, express your gratitude for all you see. Write down all the beautiful things about your current life situation.

Prayer

This is a special place of hope, victory, and healing. It is your opportunity to ask the Holy Spirit to move in certain situations and relationships. Rather than filing your complaints, tell Him how you'd like these situations and relationships to look. Jot down four specific requests below, being careful to focus on asking Him for victory in these areas instead of simply listing grievances. Be sure to pay attention over time to how things change.

1
_____

_____

_____

2
_____

_____

_____

3
_____

_____

_____

4
_____

_____

_____

Meditation

You asked the Holy Spirit to move. Now listen for God's voice. You can add music or keep it silent. Make a goal to add more time to this section over the coming weeks.

Reflection

Did you sense God speaking to you? What do you believe He is calling you to do? Do you feel excited? Conflicted? Peaceful? Was anyone brought to your mind? Did you get a new idea? Now is the time to write it all down!

Dream Life Goal

Writing your goals down each and every day creates momentum over time. Use this space to write down the Dream Life Goal or other big goal you are working toward.

_____

_____

_____

_____

_____

Affirmations

Who will you be, how will you feel, and what will your life look like when your goal is complete? Write down the affirmations that correspond to the person you are becoming and the life you are creating. When you are done, read these affirmations out loud to yourself.

I am _____

I am _____

I am _____

I am _____

I am _____

Visualization

Cement your big goal in your mind by picturing yourself achieving it. What will your life look like when your goal is completed? Notice any new details you can see today.

Dream Life Goal Action Items:

Remember, this to-do list is not about laundry, groceries, or baths for the kids. These are action-oriented steps for today that will move you toward your goals. Make sure they are all small enough and specific enough to accomplish and check off your list today.

- ☐ _____
- ☐ _____
- ☐ _____
- ☐ _____
- ☐ _____

Dream Health Action Item:

List one health-conscious thing you plan to do today. Is it to improve your water intake? Make more time for exercise? Tweak your menu or your sleep time?

- ☐ _____

Dream Relationship Action Items:

What can you do today to be more intentional about important relationships? Text your spouse? Connect with a friend? Plan special times with each of your children?

- ☐ _____
- ☐ _____
- ☐ _____
- ☐ _____

Day 17

Don't worry about anything; instead, pray about everything. Tell God what you need, and thank Him for all he has done.

Philippians 4:6, NLT

Morning Prayer

Thank You, God, for this amazing day. I love the life You've given me, and I know where I'm going because You are with me and give me strength. Thank You for the impact I am making in the world and people's lives today. Use me for Your purpose and Your glory, in Jesus' name. Amen.

Eyes Wide Open

Take a few moments to consider how God has made His presence known in your life lately. What prayers has He answered for you? How have you experienced Him in your life or surroundings?

_____

_____

_____

_____

_____

_____

Gratitude Game

Loving Who I Am

List five qualities about yourself that you appreciate and how they benefit the world.

1

2

3

4

5

Prayer

This is a special place of hope, victory, and healing. It is your opportunity to ask the Holy Spirit to move in certain situations and relationships. Rather than filing your complaints, tell Him how you'd like these situations and relationships to look. Jot down four specific requests below, being careful to focus on asking Him for victory in these areas instead of simply listing grievances. Be sure to pay attention over time to how things change.

1

2

3

4

Meditation

You asked the Holy Spirit to move. Now listen for God's voice. You can add music or keep it silent. Make a goal to add more time to this section over the coming weeks.

Reflection

Did you sense God speaking to you? What do you believe He is calling you to do? Do you feel excited? Conflicted? Peaceful? Was anyone brought to your mind? Did you get a new idea? Now is the time to write it all down!

_____

_____

_____

_____

_____

_____

_____

_____

_____

_____

_____

_____

_____

_____

_____

_____

_____

_____

Dream Life Goal

Writing your goals down each and every day creates momentum over time. Use this space to write down the Dream Life Goal or other big goal you are working toward.

_____

_____

_____

_____

_____

Affirmations

Who will you be, how will you feel, and what will your life look like when your goal is complete? Write down the affirmations that correspond to the person you are becoming and the life you are creating. When you are done, read these affirmations out loud to yourself.

I am _____

I am _____

I am _____

I am _____

I am _____

Visualization

Cement your big goal in your mind by picturing yourself achieving it. What will your life look like when your goal is completed? Notice any new details you can see today.

Dream Life Goal Action Items:

Remember, this to-do list is not about laundry, groceries, or baths for the kids. These are action-oriented steps for today that will move you toward your goals. Make sure they are all small enough and specific enough to accomplish and check off your list today.

- ☐ _____
- ☐ _____
- ☐ _____
- ☐ _____
- ☐ _____

Dream Health Action Item:

List one health-conscious thing you plan to do today. Is it to improve your water intake? Make more time for exercise? Tweak your menu or your sleep time?

- ☐ _____

Dream Relationship Action Items:

What can you do today to be more intentional about important relationships? Text your spouse? Connect with a friend? Plan special times with each of your children?

- ☐ _____
- ☐ _____
- ☐ _____
- ☐ _____

Day 18

Say this out loud: "I am grateful for all that I have, all that I am, and all that is."

Morning Prayer

Thank You, God, for this amazing day. I love the life You've given me, and I know where I'm going because You are with me and give me strength. Thank You for the impact I am making in the world and people's lives today. Use me for Your purpose and Your glory, in Jesus' name. Amen.

Eyes Wide Open

Take a few moments to consider how God has made His presence known in your life lately. What prayers has He answered for you? How have you experienced Him in your life or surroundings?

_____

_____

_____

_____

_____

_____

Gratitude Game

Four Questions

Ask yourself:
1. What touched me in the past week?
2. Who or what inspired me?
3. What made me smile?
4. What's the best thing that happened in the past seven days?

1 _____
_____
_____
_____

2 _____
_____
_____
_____

3 _____
_____
_____

4 _____
_____
_____
_____

Prayer

This is a special place of hope, victory, and healing. It is your opportunity to ask the Holy Spirit to move in certain situations and relationships. Rather than filing your complaints, tell Him how you'd like these situations and relationships to look. Jot down four specific requests below, being careful to focus on asking Him for victory in these areas instead of simply listing grievances. Be sure to pay attention over time to how things change.

1
_____
_____
_____

2
_____
_____
_____

3
_____
_____
_____

4
_____
_____
_____

Meditation

You asked the Holy Spirit to move. Now listen for God's voice. You can add music or keep it silent. Make a goal to add more time to this section over the coming weeks.

Reflection

Did you sense God speaking to you? What do you believe He is calling you to do? Do you feel excited? Conflicted? Peaceful? Was anyone brought to your mind? Did you get a new idea? Now is the time to write it all down!

_____

_____

_____

_____

_____

_____

_____

_____

_____

_____

_____

_____

_____

_____

_____

_____

_____

_____

Dream Life Goal

Writing your goals down each and every day creates momentum over time. Use this space to write down the Dream Life Goal or other big goal you are working toward.

_____

_____

_____

_____

_____

Affirmations

Who will you be, how will you feel, and what will your life look like when your goal is complete? Write down the affirmations that correspond to the person you are becoming and the life you are creating. When you are done, read these affirmations out loud to yourself.

I am _____

I am _____

I am _____

I am _____

I am _____

Visualization

Cement your big goal in your mind by picturing yourself achieving it. What will your life look like when your goal is completed? Notice any new details you can see today.

Dream Life Goal Action Items:

Remember, this to-do list is not about laundry, groceries, or baths for the kids. These are action-oriented steps for today that will move you toward your goals. Make sure they are all small enough and specific enough to accomplish and check off your list today.

- ☐ _____
- ☐ _____
- ☐ _____
- ☐ _____
- ☐ _____

Dream Health Action Item:

List one health-conscious thing you plan to do today. Is it to improve your water intake? Make more time for exercise? Tweak your menu or your sleep time?

- ☐ _____

Dream Relationship Action Items:

What can you do today to be more intentional about important relationships? Text your spouse? Connect with a friend? Plan special times with each of your children?

- ☐ _____
- ☐ _____
- ☐ _____
- ☐ _____

Day 19

My day begins and ends with gratitude and joy.

> Louise L. Hay

Morning Prayer

Thank You, God, for this amazing day. I love the life You've given me, and I know where I'm going because You are with me and give me strength. Thank You for the impact I am making in the world and people's lives today. Use me for Your purpose and Your glory, in Jesus' name. Amen.

Eyes Wide Open

Take a few moments to consider how God has made His presence known in your life lately. What prayers has He answered for you? How have you experienced Him in your life or surroundings?

_____

_____

_____

_____

_____

_____

Gratitude Game

Rearview Mirror

Describe as many happy, wonderfully awesome, super fun memories from your past that you can think of.

Include thoughts of family, vacations, friends, school experiences, hobbies, sports, etc.

Prayer

This is a special place of hope, victory, and healing. It is your opportunity to ask the Holy Spirit to move in certain situations and relationships. Rather than filing your complaints, tell Him how you'd like these situations and relationships to look. Jot down four specific requests below, being careful to focus on asking Him for victory in these areas instead of simply listing grievances. Be sure to pay attention over time to how things change.

1
_____

_____

_____

2
_____

_____

_____

3
_____

_____

_____

4
_____

_____

_____

Meditation

You asked the Holy Spirit to move. Now listen for God's voice. You can add music or keep it silent. Make a goal to add more time to this section over the coming weeks.

Reflection

Did you sense God speaking to you? What do you believe He is calling you to do? Do you feel excited? Conflicted? Peaceful? Was anyone brought to your mind? Did you get a new idea? Now is the time to write it all down!

_____

_____

_____

_____

_____

_____

_____

_____

_____

_____

_____

_____

_____

_____

_____

_____

_____

Dream Life Goal

Writing your goals down each and every day creates momentum over time. Use this space to write down the Dream Life Goal or other big goal you are working toward.

_____

_____

_____

_____

_____

Affirmations

Who will you be, how will you feel, and what will your life look like when your goal is complete? Write down the affirmations that correspond to the person you are becoming and the life you are creating. When you are done, read these affirmations out loud to yourself.

I am _____

I am _____

I am _____

I am _____

I am _____

Visualization

Cement your big goal in your mind by picturing yourself achieving it. What will your life look like when your goal is completed? Notice any new details you can see today.

Dream Life Goal Action Items:

Remember, this to-do list is not about laundry, groceries, or baths for the kids. These are action-oriented steps for today that will move you toward your goals. Make sure they are all small enough and specific enough to accomplish and check off your list today.

- ☐ _____
- ☐ _____
- ☐ _____
- ☐ _____
- ☐ _____

Dream Health Action Item:

List one health-conscious thing you plan to do today. Is it to improve your water intake? Make more time for exercise? Tweak your menu or your sleep time?

- ☐ _____

Dream Relationship Action Items:

What can you do today to be more intentional about important relationships? Text your spouse? Connect with a friend? Plan special times with each of your children?

- ☐ _____
- ☐ _____
- ☐ _____
- ☐ _____

Day 20

To be yourself in a world that is constantly trying to make you something else is the greatest accomplishment.

Ralph Waldo Emerson

Morning Prayer

Thank You, God, for this amazing day. I love the life You've given me, and I know where I'm going because You are with me and give me strength. Thank You for the impact I am making in the world and people's lives today. Use me for Your purpose and Your glory, in Jesus' name. Amen.

Eyes Wide Open

Take a few moments to consider how God has made His presence known in your life lately. What prayers has He answered for you? How have you experienced Him in your life or surroundings?

_____

_____

_____

_____

_____

_____

Gratitude Game
Playing Favorites

Name someone for whom you are thankful, something for whom you are thankful, somewhere for which you are grateful, a food you especially love to eat, and a book you are glad someone wrote.

Tell why these people and things are special to you.

Prayer

This is a special place of hope, victory, and healing. It is your opportunity to ask the Holy Spirit to move in certain situations and relationships. Rather than filing your complaints, tell Him how you'd like these situations and relationships to look. Jot down four specific requests below, being careful to focus on asking Him for victory in these areas instead of simply listing grievances. Be sure to pay attention over time to how things change.

1
_____
_____
_____

2
_____
_____
_____

3
_____
_____
_____

4
_____
_____
_____

Meditation

You asked the Holy Spirit to move. Now listen for God's voice. You can add music or keep it silent. Make a goal to add more time to this section over the coming weeks.

Reflection

Did you sense God speaking to you? What do you believe He is calling you to do? Do you feel excited? Conflicted? Peaceful? Was anyone brought to your mind? Did you get a new idea? Now is the time to write it all down!

Dream Life Goal

Writing your goals down each and every day creates momentum over time. Use this space to write down the Dream Life Goal or other big goal you are working toward.

_____

_____

_____

_____

_____

Affirmations

Who will you be, how will you feel, and what will your life look like when your goal is complete? Write down the affirmations that correspond to the person you are becoming and the life you are creating. When you are done, read these affirmations out loud to yourself.

I am _____

I am _____

I am _____

I am _____

I am _____

Visualization

Cement your big goal in your mind by picturing yourself achieving it. What will your life look like when your goal is completed? Notice any new details you can see today.

Dream Life Goal Action Items:

Remember, this to-do list is not about laundry, groceries, or baths for the kids. These are action-oriented steps for today that will move you toward your goals. Make sure they are all small enough and specific enough to accomplish and check off your list today.

- ☐ _____
- ☐ _____
- ☐ _____
- ☐ _____
- ☐ _____

Dream Health Action Item:

List one health-conscious thing you plan to do today. Is it to improve your water intake? Make more time for exercise? Tweak your menu or your sleep time?

- ☐ _____

Dream Relationship Action Items:

What can you do today to be more intentional about important relationships? Text your spouse? Connect with a friend? Plan special times with each of your children?

- ☐ _____
- ☐ _____
- ☐ _____
- ☐ _____

Day 21

Imagine with all your mind. Believe with all your heart. Achieve with all your might.

Morning Prayer

Thank You, God, for this amazing day. I love the life You've given me, and I know where I'm going because You are with me and give me strength. Thank You for the impact I am making in the world and people's lives today. Use me for Your purpose and Your glory, in Jesus' name. Amen.

Eyes Wide Open

Take a few moments to consider how God has made His presence known in your life lately. What prayers has He answered for you? How have you experienced Him in your life or surroundings?

_____

_____

_____

_____

_____

_____

Gratitude Game

Joy Review

What five things are you ferociously grateful for today, and why? Include the little things that made you smile in the past twenty-four hours.

1

2

3

4

5

Prayer

This is a special place of hope, victory, and healing. It is your opportunity to ask the Holy Spirit to move in certain situations and relationships. Rather than filing your complaints, tell Him how you'd like these situations and relationships to look. Jot down four specific requests below, being careful to focus on asking Him for victory in these areas instead of simply listing grievances. Be sure to pay attention over time to how things change.

1

_

_

2

_

_

3

_

_

4

_

_

Meditation

You asked the Holy Spirit to move. Now listen for God's voice. You can add music or keep it silent. Make a goal to add more time to this section over the coming weeks.

Reflection

Did you sense God speaking to you? What do you believe He is calling you to do? Do you feel excited? Conflicted? Peaceful? Was anyone brought to your mind? Did you get a new idea? Now is the time to write it all down!

_____

_____

_____

_____

_____

_____

_____

_____

_____

_____

_____

_____

_____

_____

_____

_____

_____

Dream Life Goal

Writing your goals down each and every day creates momentum over time. Use this space to write down the Dream Life Goal or other big goal you are working toward.

_____

_____

_____

_____

_____

Affirmations

Who will you be, how will you feel, and what will your life look like when your goal is complete? Write down the affirmations that correspond to the person you are becoming and the life you are creating. When you are done, read these affirmations out loud to yourself.

I am _____

I am _____

I am _____

I am _____

I am _____

Visualization

Cement your big goal in your mind by picturing yourself achieving it. What will your life look like when your goal is completed? Notice any new details you can see today.

Dream Life Goal Action Items:

Remember, this to-do list is not about laundry, groceries, or baths for the kids. These are action-oriented steps for today that will move you toward your goals. Make sure they are all small enough and specific enough to accomplish and check off your list today.

- [ ] _____
- [ ] _____
- [ ] _____
- [ ] _____
- [ ] _____

Dream Health Action Item:

List one health-conscious thing you plan to do today. Is it to improve your water intake? Make more time for exercise? Tweak your menu or your sleep time?

- [ ] _____

Dream Relationship Action Items:

What can you do today to be more intentional about important relationships? Text your spouse? Connect with a friend? Plan special times with each of your children?

- [ ] _____
- [ ] _____
- [ ] _____
- [ ] _____

Day 22

Work like you don't need the money. Love like you've never been hurt. Dance like nobody's watching.

Satchell Paige

Morning Prayer

Thank You, God, for this amazing day. I love the life You've given me, and I know where I'm going because You are with me and give me strength. Thank You for the impact I am making in the world and people's lives today. Use me for Your purpose and Your glory, in Jesus' name. Amen.

Eyes Wide Open

Take a few moments to consider how God has made His presence known in your life lately. What prayers has He answered for you? How have you experienced Him in your life or surroundings?

_____

_____

_____

_____

_____

_____

Gratitude Game

High Times!

Name two or three pivotal moments in your life and describe how they positively impacted you.

When you look back, why were they so significant, and how did they influence you to become who you are today?

Prayer

This is a special place of hope, victory, and healing. It is your opportunity to ask the Holy Spirit to move in certain situations and relationships. Rather than filing your complaints, tell Him how you'd like these situations and relationships to look. Jot down four specific requests below, being careful to focus on asking Him for victory in these areas instead of simply listing grievances. Be sure to pay attention over time to how things change.

1
_____

_____

_____

2
_____

_____

_____

3
_____

_____

_____

4
_____

_____

_____

Meditation

You asked the Holy Spirit to move. Now listen for God's voice. You can add music or keep it silent. Make a goal to add more time to this section over the coming weeks.

Reflection

Did you sense God speaking to you? What do you believe He is calling you to do? Do you feel excited? Conflicted? Peaceful? Was anyone brought to your mind? Did you get a new idea? Now is the time to write it all down!

Dream Life Goal

Writing your goals down each and every day creates momentum over time. Use this space to write down the Dream Life Goal or other big goal you are working toward.

_____

_____

_____

_____

_____

_____

Affirmations

Who will you be, how will you feel, and what will your life look like when your goal is complete? Write down the affirmations that correspond to the person you are becoming and the life you are creating. When you are done, read these affirmations out loud to yourself.

I am _____

I am _____

I am _____

I am _____

I am _____

Visualization

Cement your big goal in your mind by picturing yourself achieving it. What will your life look like when your goal is completed? Notice any new details you can see today.

Dream Life Goal Action Items:

Remember, this to-do list is not about laundry, groceries, or baths for the kids. These are action-oriented steps for today that will move you toward your goals. Make sure they are all small enough and specific enough to accomplish and check off your list today.

- [ ] _____
- [ ] _____
- [ ] _____
- [ ] _____
- [ ] _____

Dream Health Action Item:

List one health-conscious thing you plan to do today. Is it to improve your water intake? Make more time for exercise? Tweak your menu or your sleep time?

- [ ] _____

Dream Relationship Action Items:

What can you do today to be more intentional about important relationships? Text your spouse? Connect with a friend? Plan special times with each of your children?

- [ ] _____
- [ ] _____
- [ ] _____
- [ ] _____

Day 23

Gratitude makes sense of our past, brings peace for today, and creates a vision for tomorrow.

Melody Beattie

Morning Prayer

Thank You, God, for this amazing day. I love the life You've given me, and I know where I'm going because You are with me and give me strength. Thank You for the impact I am making in the world and people's lives today. Use me for Your purpose and Your glory, in Jesus' name. Amen.

Eyes Wide Open

Take a few moments to consider how God has made His presence known in your life lately. What prayers has He answered for you? How have you experienced Him in your life or surroundings?

_____

_____

_____

_____

_____

_____

Gratitude Game

God Is All Around

Think back to a time when you saw God move in your life right when you needed it but in a way you didn't expect. Describe the experience as if it were happening to you again today. (For example, you could say something like, "I have been looking for a camp to go to this summer, and the perfect one showed up in my e-mail today! God always seems to show up exactly when I need Him.")

Prayer

This is a special place of hope, victory, and healing. It is your opportunity to ask the Holy Spirit to move in certain situations and relationships. Rather than filing your complaints, tell Him how you'd like these situations and relationships to look. Jot down four specific requests below, being careful to focus on asking Him for victory in these areas instead of simply listing grievances. Be sure to pay attention over time to how things change.

1
_____
_____
_____

2
_____
_____
_____

3
_____
_____
_____

4
_____
_____
_____

Meditation

You asked the Holy Spirit to move. Now listen for God's voice. You can add music or keep it silent. Make a goal to add more time to this section over the coming weeks.

Reflection

Did you sense God speaking to you? What do you believe He is calling you to do? Do you feel excited? Conflicted? Peaceful? Was anyone brought to your mind? Did you get a new idea? Now is the time to write it all down!

Dream Life Goal

Writing your goals down each and every day creates momentum over time. Use this space to write down the Dream Life Goal or other big goal you are working toward.

_____

_____

_____

_____

_____

_____

Affirmations

Who will you be, how will you feel, and what will your life look like when your goal is complete? Write down the affirmations that correspond to the person you are becoming and the life you are creating. When you are done, read these affirmations out loud to yourself.

I am _____

I am _____

I am _____

I am _____

I am _____

Visualization

Cement your big goal in your mind by picturing yourself achieving it. What will your life look like when your goal is completed? Notice any new details you can see today.

Dream Life Goal Action Items:

Remember, this to-do list is not about laundry, groceries, or baths for the kids. These are action-oriented steps for today that will move you toward your goals. Make sure they are all small enough and specific enough to accomplish and check off your list today.

- [ ] _____
- [ ] _____
- [ ] _____
- [ ] _____
- [ ] _____

Dream Health Action Item:

List one health-conscious thing you plan to do today. Is it to improve your water intake? Make more time for exercise? Tweak your menu or your sleep time?

- [ ] _____

Dream Relationship Action Items:

What can you do today to be more intentional about important relationships? Text your spouse? Connect with a friend? Plan special times with each of your children?

- [ ] _____
- [ ] _____
- [ ] _____
- [ ] _____

Day 24

Let us always meet each other with smile, for the smile is the beginning of love.

Mother Teresa

Morning Prayer

Thank You, God, for this amazing day. I love the life You've given me, and I know where I'm going because You are with me and give me strength. Thank You for the impact I am making in the world and people's lives today. Use me for Your purpose and Your glory, in Jesus' name. Amen.

Eyes Wide Open

Take a few moments to consider how God has made His presence known in your life lately. What prayers has He answered for you? How have you experienced Him in your life or surroundings?

_____

_____

_____

_____

_____

_____

Gratitude Game
Peak Experience

Take a deep breath, think about a peak experience from the past year—a high moment in your life, one that was filled with great joy and overflowed with positive emotion—and then write about it in the present tense.

Describe the experience itself, as well as what made it special and why you are grateful for it.

Prayer

This is a special place of hope, victory, and healing. It is your opportunity to ask the Holy Spirit to move in certain situations and relationships. Rather than filing your complaints, tell Him how you'd like these situations and relationships to look. Jot down four specific requests below, being careful to focus on asking Him for victory in these areas instead of simply listing grievances. Be sure to pay attention over time to how things change.

1

2

3

4

Meditation

You asked the Holy Spirit to move. Now listen for God's voice. You can add music or keep it silent. Make a goal to add more time to this section over the coming weeks.

Reflection

Did you sense God speaking to you? What do you believe He is calling you to do? Do you feel excited? Conflicted? Peaceful? Was anyone brought to your mind? Did you get a new idea? Now is the time to write it all down!

Dream Life Goal

Writing your goals down each and every day creates momentum over time. Use this space to write down the Dream Life Goal or other big goal you are working toward.

_____

_____

_____

_____

_____

Affirmations

Who will you be, how will you feel, and what will your life look like when your goal is complete? Write down the affirmations that correspond to the person you are becoming and the life you are creating. When you are done, read these affirmations out loud to yourself.

I am _____

I am _____

I am _____

I am _____

I am _____

Visualization

Cement your big goal in your mind by picturing yourself achieving it. What will your life look like when your goal is completed? Notice any new details you can see today.

Dream Life Goal Action Items:

Remember, this to-do list is not about laundry, groceries, or baths for the kids. These are action-oriented steps for today that will move you toward your goals. Make sure they are all small enough and specific enough to accomplish and check off your list today.

- [ ] _____
- [ ] _____
- [ ] _____
- [ ] _____
- [ ] _____

Dream Health Action Item:

List one health-conscious thing you plan to do today. Is it to improve your water intake? Make more time for exercise? Tweak your menu or your sleep time?

- [ ] _____

Dream Relationship Action Items:

What can you do today to be more intentional about important relationships? Text your spouse? Connect with a friend? Plan special times with each of your children?

- [ ] _____
- [ ] _____
- [ ] _____
- [ ] _____

Day 25

Setting goals is the first step in turning the invisible into the visible.

Tony Robbins

Morning Prayer

Thank You, God, for this amazing day. I love the life You've given me, and I know where I'm going because You are with me and give me strength. Thank You for the impact I am making in the world and people's lives today. Use me for Your purpose and Your glory, in Jesus' name. Amen.

Eyes Wide Open

Take a few moments to consider how God has made His presence known in your life lately. What prayers has He answered for you? How have you experienced Him in your life or surroundings?

_____

_____

_____

_____

_____

Gratitude Game

Start a Gratitude Jar!

Braintstorm a list of all the amazing things you can think of about your life, your family, and your current situation.

Later, grab a jar and some small slips of paper. Transfer some or all of what you wrote down to those slips of paper and add them to the jar. From now on, every day make it a point to write down something fun, special, beautiful that happened that day and add it to the jar. At the end of the year you can go through your gratitude jar as a way of remembering what an amazing year you had.

Prayer

This is a special place of hope, victory, and healing. It is your opportunity to ask the Holy Spirit to move in certain situations and relationships. Rather than filing your complaints, tell Him how you'd like these situations and relationships to look. Jot down four specific requests below, being careful to focus on asking Him for victory in these areas instead of simply listing grievances. Be sure to pay attention over time to how things change.

1

2

3

4

Meditation

You asked the Holy Spirit to move. Now listen for God's voice. You can add music or keep it silent. Make a goal to add more time to this section over the coming weeks.

Reflection

Did you sense God speaking to you? What do you believe He is calling you to do? Do you feel excited? Conflicted? Peaceful? Was anyone brought to your mind? Did you get a new idea? Now is the time to write it all down!

Dream Life Goal

Writing your goals down each and every day creates momentum over time. Use this space to write down the Dream Life Goal or other big goal you are working toward.

_____

_____

_____

_____

_____

Affirmations

Who will you be, how will you feel, and what will your life look like when your goal is complete? Write down the affirmations that correspond to the person you are becoming and the life you are creating. When you are done, read these affirmations out loud to yourself.

I am _____

I am _____

I am _____

I am _____

I am _____

Visualization

Cement your big goal in your mind by picturing yourself achieving it. What will your life look like when your goal is completed? Notice any new details you can see today.

Dream Life Goal Action Items:

Remember, this to-do list is not about laundry, groceries, or baths for the kids. These are action-oriented steps for today that will move you toward your goals. Make sure they are all small enough and specific enough to accomplish and check off your list today.

☐ _____

☐ _____

☐ _____

☐ _____

☐ _____

Dream Health Action Item:

List one health-conscious thing you plan to do today. Is it to improve your water intake? Make more time for exercise? Tweak your menu or your sleep time?

☐ _____

Dream Relationship Action Items:

What can you do today to be more intentional about important relationships? Text your spouse? Connect with a friend? Plan special times with each of your children?

☐ _____

☐ _____

☐ _____

☐ _____

Day 26

It's impossible to feel grateful and anxious simultaneously. It's impossible to feel grateful and angry simultaneously. It's impossible to feel grateful and bitter simultaneously.

Rachel Hollis
Girl, Wash Your Face

Morning Prayer

Thank You, God, for this amazing day. I love the life You've given me, and I know where I'm going because You are with me and give me strength. Thank You for the impact I am making in the world and people's lives today. Use me for Your purpose and Your glory, in Jesus' name. Amen.

Eyes Wide Open

Take a few moments to consider how God has made His presence known in your life lately. What prayers has He answered for you? How have you experienced Him in your life or surroundings?

_____

_____

_____

_____

_____

_____

Gratitude Game
Strengths Bombardment

The more we take notice of the good in others, the more readily we will see those qualities in them.

Today, write down ten qualities about yourself and five about your significant other and anyone else in your life.

Yourself

_____

_____

_____

_____

_____

_____

_____

_____

Significant Other

_____

_____

_____

_____

Others In Your Life

_____

_____

_____

_____

Prayer

This is a special place of hope, victory, and healing. It is your opportunity to ask the Holy Spirit to move in certain situations and relationships. Rather than filing your complaints, tell Him how you'd like these situations and relationships to look. Jot down four specific requests below, being careful to focus on asking Him for victory in these areas instead of simply listing grievances. Be sure to pay attention over time to how things change.

1

_____

_____

_____

2

_____

_____

_____

3

_____

_____

_____

4

_____

_____

_____

Meditation

You asked the Holy Spirit to move. Now listen for God's voice. You can add music or keep it silent. Make a goal to add more time to this section over the coming weeks.

Reflection

Did you sense God speaking to you? What do you believe He is calling you to do? Do you feel excited? Conflicted? Peaceful? Was anyone brought to your mind? Did you get a new idea? Now is the time to write it all down!

_____

_____

_____

_____

_____

_____

_____

_____

_____

_____

_____

_____

_____

_____

_____

_____

_____

_____

Dream Life Goal

Writing your goals down each and every day creates momentum over time. Use this space to write down the Dream Life Goal or other big goal you are working toward.

_____

_____

_____

_____

_____

_____

Affirmations

Who will you be, how will you feel, and what will your life look like when your goal is complete? Write down the affirmations that correspond to the person you are becoming and the life you are creating. When you are done, read these affirmations out loud to yourself.

I am _____

I am _____

I am _____

I am _____

I am _____

Visualization

Cement your big goal in your mind by picturing yourself achieving it. What will your life look like when your goal is completed? Notice any new details you can see today.

Dream Life Goal Action Items:

Remember, this to-do list is not about laundry, groceries, or baths for the kids. These are action-oriented steps for today that will move you toward your goals. Make sure they are all small enough and specific enough to accomplish and check off your list today.

- ☐ _____
- ☐ _____
- ☐ _____
- ☐ _____
- ☐ _____

Dream Health Action Item:

List one health-conscious thing you plan to do today. Is it to improve your water intake? Make more time for exercise? Tweak your menu or your sleep time?

- ☐ _____

Dream Relationship Action Items:

What can you do today to be more intentional about important relationships? Text your spouse? Connect with a friend? Plan special times with each of your children?

- ☐ _____
- ☐ _____
- ☐ _____
- ☐ _____

Day 27

Repeat three times: "I love where I am, and I know where I am going."

Morning Prayer

Thank You, God, for this amazing day. I love the life You've given me, and I know where I'm going because You are with me and give me strength. Thank You for the impact I am making in the world and people's lives today. Use me for Your purpose and Your glory, in Jesus' name. Amen.

Eyes Wide Open

Take a few moments to consider how God has made His presence known in your life lately. What prayers has He answered for you? How have you experienced Him in your life or surroundings?

_____

_____

_____

_____

_____

_____

Gratitude Game
Love Where You Are

Deep breath. Look around you.

What do you appreciate about your home, your yard, your car, your family, and your current situation? Write down all that you appreciate about your life today.

Prayer

This is a special place of hope, victory, and healing. It is your opportunity to ask the Holy Spirit to move in certain situations and relationships. Rather than filing your complaints, tell Him how you'd like these situations and relationships to look. Jot down four specific requests below, being careful to focus on asking Him for victory in these areas instead of simply listing grievances. Be sure to pay attention over time to how things change.

1

_____

_____

2

_____

_____

3

_____

_____

4

_____

_____

Meditation

You asked the Holy Spirit to move. Now listen for God's voice. You can add music or keep it silent. Make a goal to add more time to this section over the coming weeks.

Reflection

Did you sense God speaking to you? What do you believe He is calling you to do? Do you feel excited? Conflicted? Peaceful? Was anyone brought to your mind? Did you get a new idea? Now is the time to write it all down!

Day 27

Dream Life Goal

Writing your goals down each and every day creates momentum over time. Use this space to write down the Dream Life Goal or other big goal you are working toward.

_____

_____

_____

_____

_____

_____

Affirmations

Who will you be, how will you feel, and what will your life look like when your goal is complete? Write down the affirmations that correspond to the person you are becoming and the life you are creating. When you are done, read these affirmations out loud to yourself.

I am _____

I am _____

I am _____

I am _____

I am _____

Visualization

Cement your big goal in your mind by picturing yourself achieving it. What will your life look like when your goal is completed? Notice any new details you can see today.

Dream Life Goal Action Items:

Remember, this to-do list is not about laundry, groceries, or baths for the kids. These are action-oriented steps for today that will move you toward your goals. Make sure they are all small enough and specific enough to accomplish and check off your list today.

- [ ] _____
- [ ] _____
- [ ] _____
- [ ] _____
- [ ] _____

Dream Health Action Item:

List one health-conscious thing you plan to do today. Is it to improve your water intake? Make more time for exercise? Tweak your menu or your sleep time?

- [ ] _____

Dream Relationship Action Items:

What can you do today to be more intentional about important relationships? Text your spouse? Connect with a friend? Plan special times with each of your children?

- [ ] _____
- [ ] _____
- [ ] _____
- [ ] _____

Day 28

Your personal vision is a picture of your future that produces passion.

Morning Prayer

Thank You, God, for this amazing day. I love the life You've given me, and I know where I'm going because You are with me and give me strength. Thank You for the impact I am making in the world and people's lives today. Use me for Your purpose and Your glory, in Jesus' name. Amen.

Eyes Wide Open

Take a few moments to consider how God has made His presence known in your life lately. What prayers has He answered for you? How have you experienced Him in your life or surroundings?

_____

_____

_____

_____

_____

Gratitude Game
Picture Perfect

Think about your ideal day, a day in which every area of your life is functioning in the best scenario you can imagine. On that perfect day, how would you wake up, what would you do, who would you be with, and how would you feel?

There is no reason to be reasonable here. Dream freely and think about what you really want to feel, experience, be with, and spend your time.

Spend time writing down all the details of your day, and then picture yourself living it.

Prayer

This is a special place of hope, victory, and healing. It is your opportunity to ask the Holy Spirit to move in certain situations and relationships. Rather than filing your complaints, tell Him how you'd like these situations and relationships to look. Jot down four specific requests below, being careful to focus on asking Him for victory in these areas instead of simply listing grievances. Be sure to pay attention over time to how things change.

1 _____

_____

_____

2 _____

_____

_____

3 _____

_____

_____

4 _____

_____

_____

Meditation

You asked the Holy Spirit to move. Now listen for God's voice. You can add music or keep it silent. Make a goal to add more time to this section over the coming weeks.

Reflection

Did you sense God speaking to you? What do you believe He is calling you to do? Do you feel excited? Conflicted? Peaceful? Was anyone brought to your mind? Did you get a new idea? Now is the time to write it all down!

Dream Life Goal

Writing your goals down each and every day creates momentum over time. Use this space to write down the Dream Life Goal or other big goal you are working toward.

_____

_____

_____

_____

_____

_____

Affirmations

Who will you be, how will you feel, and what will your life look like when your goal is complete? Write down the affirmations that correspond to the person you are becoming and the life you are creating. When you are done, read these affirmations out loud to yourself.

I am _____

I am _____

I am _____

I am _____

I am _____

Visualization

Cement your big goal in your mind by picturing yourself achieving it. What will your life look like when your goal is completed? Notice any new details you can see today.

Dream Life Goal Action Items:

Remember, this to-do list is not about laundry, groceries, or baths for the kids. These are action-oriented steps for today that will move you toward your goals. Make sure they are all small enough and specific enough to accomplish and check off your list today.

- [ ] _____
- [ ] _____
- [ ] _____
- [ ] _____
- [ ] _____

Dream Health Action Item:

List one health-conscious thing you plan to do today. Is it to improve your water intake? Make more time for exercise? Tweak your menu or your sleep time?

- [ ] _____

Dream Relationship Action Items:

What can you do today to be more intentional about important relationships? Text your spouse? Connect with a friend? Plan special times with each of your children?

- [ ] _____
- [ ] _____
- [ ] _____
- [ ] _____

Day 29

Your positive action combined with positive thinking results in success.
Shiv Khera

Morning Prayer

Thank You, God, for this amazing day. I love the life You've given me, and I know where I'm going because You are with me and give me strength. Thank You for the impact I am making in the world and people's lives today. Use me for Your purpose and Your glory, in Jesus' name. Amen.

Eyes Wide Open

Take a few moments to consider how God has made His presence known in your life lately. What prayers has He answered for you? How have you experienced Him in your life or surroundings?

_____

_____

_____

_____

_____

_____

Gratitude Game

Laughter

Think about when you laughed the biggest, longest, belly laugh you have ever had.

Describe that situation. Who was there with you, and what about it was so entertaining?

Prayer

This is a special place of hope, victory, and healing. It is your opportunity to ask the Holy Spirit to move in certain situations and relationships. Rather than filing your complaints, tell Him how you'd like these situations and relationships to look. Jot down four specific requests below, being careful to focus on asking Him for victory in these areas instead of simply listing grievances. Be sure to pay attention over time to how things change.

1 _____

_____

_____

2 _____

_____

_____

3 _____

_____

_____

4 _____

_____

_____

Meditation

You asked the Holy Spirit to move. Now listen for God's voice. You can add music or keep it silent. Make a goal to add more time to this section over the coming weeks.

Reflection

Did you sense God speaking to you? What do you believe He is calling you to do? Do you feel excited? Conflicted? Peaceful? Was anyone brought to your mind? Did you get a new idea? Now is the time to write it all down!

_____

_____

_____

_____

_____

_____

_____

_____

_____

_____

_____

_____

_____

_____

_____

_____

_____

_____

_____

_____

Dream Life Goal

Writing your goals down each and every day creates momentum over time. Use this space to write down the Dream Life Goal or other big goal you are working toward.

_____

_____

_____

_____

_____

_____

Affirmations

Who will you be, how will you feel, and what will your life look like when your goal is complete? Write down the affirmations that correspond to the person you are becoming and the life you are creating. When you are done, read these affirmations out loud to yourself.

I am _____

I am _____

I am _____

I am _____

I am _____

Visualization

Cement your big goal in your mind by picturing yourself achieving it. What will your life look like when your goal is completed? Notice any new details you can see today.

Dream Life Goal Action Items:

Remember, this to-do list is not about laundry, groceries, or baths for the kids. These are action-oriented steps for today that will move you toward your goals. Make sure they are all small enough and specific enough to accomplish and check off your list today.

- [ ] _____
- [ ] _____
- [ ] _____
- [ ] _____
- [ ] _____

Dream Health Action Item:

List one health-conscious thing you plan to do today. Is it to improve your water intake? Make more time for exercise? Tweak your menu or your sleep time?

- [ ] _____

Dream Relationship Action Items:

What can you do today to be more intentional about important relationships? Text your spouse? Connect with a friend? Plan special times with each of your children?

- [ ] _____
- [ ] _____
- [ ] _____
- [ ] _____

Day 30

Love is old. Love is new. Love is all.
Love is you.

The Beatles

Morning Prayer

Thank You, God, for this amazing day. I love the life You've given me, and I know where I'm going because You are with me and give me strength. Thank You for the impact I am making in the world and people's lives today. Use me for Your purpose and Your glory, in Jesus' name. Amen.

Eyes Wide Open

Take a few moments to consider how God has made His presence known in your life lately. What prayers has He answered for you? How have you experienced Him in your life or surroundings?

_____

_____

_____

_____

_____

_____

_____

Gratitude Game
Thank You, Everyone

Today your eyes are wide open to everyone around you.

Take a few moments to think about the friends, family members, teachers, and others you are grateful for. Write down who you want to thank and why.

Then take the time to send a thank-you text to each of them letting them know why you are grateful for them.

Prayer

This is a special place of hope, victory, and healing. It is your opportunity to ask the Holy Spirit to move in certain situations and relationships. Rather than filing your complaints, tell Him how you'd like these situations and relationships to look. Jot down four specific requests below, being careful to focus on asking Him for victory in these areas instead of simply listing grievances. Be sure to pay attention over time to how things change.

1 _____

_____

_____

2 _____

_____

_____

3 _____

_____

_____

4 _____

_____

_____

Meditation

You asked the Holy Spirit to move. Now listen for God's voice. You can add music or keep it silent. Make a goal to add more time to this section over the coming weeks.

Reflection

Did you sense God speaking to you? What do you believe He is calling you to do? Do you feel excited? Conflicted? Peaceful? Was anyone brought to your mind? Did you get a new idea? Now is the time to write it all down!

_____

_____

_____

_____

_____

_____

_____

_____

_____

_____

_____

_____

_____

_____

_____

_____

_____

_____

Dream Life Goal

Writing your goals down each and every day creates momentum over time. Use this space to write down the Dream Life Goal or other big goal you are working toward.

_____

_____

_____

_____

_____

_____

Affirmations

Who will you be, how will you feel, and what will your life look like when your goal is complete? Write down the affirmations that correspond to the person you are becoming and the life you are creating. When you are done, read these affirmations out loud to yourself.

I am _____

I am _____

I am _____

I am _____

I am _____

Visualization

Cement your big goal in your mind by picturing yourself achieving it. What will your life look like when your goal is completed? Notice any new details you can see today.

Dream Life Goal Action Items:

Remember, this to-do list is not about laundry, groceries, or baths for the kids. These are action-oriented steps for today that will move you toward your goals. Make sure they are all small enough and specific enough to accomplish and check off your list today.

- ☐ _____
- ☐ _____
- ☐ _____
- ☐ _____
- ☐ _____

Dream Health Action Item:

List one health-conscious thing you plan to do today. Is it to improve your water intake? Make more time for exercise? Tweak your menu or your sleep time?

- ☐ _____

Dream Relationship Action Items:

What can you do today to be more intentional about important relationships? Text your spouse? Connect with a friend? Plan special times with each of your children?

- ☐ _____
- ☐ _____
- ☐ _____
- ☐ _____

> Life begins each morning.
> Joel Osteen

Conclusion

Congratulations! You are thirty days closer to living your Dream Life!

During the last month we have spent together, you have made and cemented habits that will change your life forever. Keep this going. This new habit is sending you down a new path--a path that leads toward success. Don't stop now. Continue connecting with your Dream Life Goals daily and taking time each morning to determine a plan of action and execute it. If you need to, pick up another copy of this journal and go through it again. Remember, what the mind sees, the body follows, and consistency will create and rapidly build momentum.

I am so excited you have chosen to allow me to make this journey with you. If you want continued support on your journey, follow me on YouTube or subscribe to my podcast, Dream Cast. You can also visit DreamLifeToolKit.com for additional resources to help you on your way.

Now, keep up the momentum and continue to dream big!